This Plan Book Belongs To:

_____

Grade Level:_____

School Year:_____

Weekly Overview

	Monday	Tuesday	Wednesday	Thursday	Friday
Group 1					
Group 2					
Group 3					
Group 4					
Group 5					

Weekly Overview

	Monday	Tuesday	Wednesday	Thursday	Friday
Group 1					
Group 2					
Group 3					
Group 4					
Group 5					

Weekly Overview

	Monday	Tuesday	Wednesday	Thursday	Friday
Group 1					
Group 2					
Group 3					
Group 4					
Group 5					

Weekly Overview

	Monday	Tuesday	Wednesday	Thursday	Friday
Group 1					
Group 2					
Group 3					
Group 4					
Group 5					

Weekly Overview

	Monday	Tuesday	Wednesday	Thursday	Friday
Group 1					
Group 2					
Group 3					
Group 4					
Group 5					

Weekly Overview

	Monday	Tuesday	Wednesday	Thursday	Friday
Group 1					
Group 2					
Group 3					
Group 4					
Group 5					

Weekly Overview

	Monday	Tuesday	Wednesday	Thursday	Friday
Group 1					
Group 2					
Group 3					
Group 4					
Group 5					

Weekly Overview

	Monday	Tuesday	Wednesday	Thursday	Friday
Group 1					
Group 2					
Group 3					
Group 4					
Group 5					

Weekly Overview

	Monday	Tuesday	Wednesday	Thursday	Friday
Group 1					
Group 2					
Group 3					
Group 4					
Group 5					

Weekly Overview

	Monday	Tuesday	Wednesday	Thursday	Friday
Group 1					
Group 2					
Group 3					
Group 4					
Group 5					

Weekly Overview

	Monday	Tuesday	Wednesday	Thursday	Friday
Group 1					
Group 2					
Group 3					
Group 4					
Group 5					

Weekly Overview

	Monday	Tuesday	Wednesday	Thursday	Friday
Group 1					
Group 2					
Group 3					
Group 4					
Group 5					

Weekly Overview

	Monday	Tuesday	Wednesday	Thursday	Friday
Group 1					
Group 2					
Group 3					
Group 4					
Group 5					

Weekly Overview

	Monday	Tuesday	Wednesday	Thursday	Friday
Group 1					
Group 2					
Group 3					
Group 4					
Group 5					

Weekly Overview

	Monday	Tuesday	Wednesday	Thursday	Friday
Group 1					
Group 2					
Group 3					
Group 4					
Group 5					

Weekly Overview

	Monday	Tuesday	Wednesday	Thursday	Friday
Group 1					
Group 2					
Group 3					
Group 4					
Group 5					

Weekly Overview

	Monday	Tuesday	Wednesday	Thursday	Friday
Group 1					
Group 2					
Group 3					
Group 4					
Group 5					

Weekly Overview

	Monday	Tuesday	Wednesday	Thursday	Friday
Group 1					
Group 2					
Group 3					
Group 4					
Group 5					

Weekly Overview

	Monday	Tuesday	Wednesday	Thursday	Friday
Group 1					
Group 2					
Group 3					
Group 4					
Group 5					

Weekly Overview

	Monday	Tuesday	Wednesday	Thursday	Friday
Group 1					
Group 2					
Group 3					
Group 4					
Group 5					

Lesson Plan

Group: Date:

Book Title: Level:

Word Work:

Teaching Point/Strategy: Vocabulary:

Before Reading:

During Reading:

After Reading:

Other:

Notes

Student Name:	Notes:
Skills to work on:	
Student Name:	Notes:
Skills to work on:	
Student Name:	Notes:
Skills to work on:	
Student Name:	Notes:
Skills to work on:	
Student Name:	Notes:
Skills to work on:	

Lesson Plan

Group:	Date:

Book Title:	Level:

Word Work:

Teaching Point/Strategy:	Vocabulary:

Before Reading:

During Reading:

After Reading:

Other:

Notes

Student Name:	Notes:
Skills to work on:	
Student Name:	Notes:
Skills to work on:	
Student Name:	Notes:
Skills to work on:	
Student Name:	Notes:
Skills to work on:	
Student Name:	Notes:
Skills to work on:	

Lesson Plan

Group:	Date:

Book Title:	Level:

Word Work:

Teaching Point/Strategy:	Vocabulary:

Before Reading:

During Reading:

After Reading:

Other:

Notes

Student Name:	Notes:
Skills to work on:	
Student Name:	Notes:
Skills to work on:	
Student Name:	Notes:
Skills to work on:	
Student Name:	Notes:
Skills to work on:	
Student Name:	Notes:
Skills to work on:	

Lesson Plan

Group:	Date:
Book Title:	Level:

Word Work:

Teaching Point/Strategy:	Vocabulary:

Before Reading:

During Reading:

After Reading:

Other:

Notes

Student Name: Skills to work on:	Notes:
Student Name: Skills to work on:	Notes:
Student Name: Skills to work on:	Notes:
Student Name: Skills to work on:	Notes:
Student Name: Skills to work on:	Notes:

Lesson Plan

Group: Date:

Book Title: Level:

Word Work:

Teaching Point/Strategy: Vocabulary:

Before Reading:

During Reading:

After Reading:

Other:

Notes

Student Name:	Notes:
Skills to work on:	
Student Name:	Notes:
Skills to work on:	
Student Name:	Notes:
Skills to work on:	
Student Name:	Notes:
Skills to work on:	
Student Name:	Notes:
Skills to work on:	

Lesson Plan

Group:	Date:
Book Title:	Level:

Word Work:

Teaching Point/Strategy:	Vocabulary:

Before Reading:

During Reading:

After Reading:

Other:

Notes

Student Name: Skills to work on:	Notes:
Student Name: Skills to work on:	Notes:
Student Name: Skills to work on:	Notes:
Student Name: Skills to work on:	Notes:
Student Name: Skills to work on:	Notes:

Lesson Plan

Group:	Date:

Book Title: Level:

Word Work:

Teaching Point/Strategy:	Vocabulary:

Before Reading:

During Reading:

After Reading:

Other:

Notes

Student Name: Skills to work on:	Notes:
Student Name: Skills to work on:	Notes:
Student Name: Skills to work on:	Notes:
Student Name: Skills to work on:	Notes:
Student Name: Skills to work on:	Notes:

Lesson Plan

Group:	Date:
Book Title:	**Level:**

Word Work:

Teaching Point/Strategy:	**Vocabulary:**

Before Reading:

During Reading:

After Reading:

Other:

Notes

Student Name:	Notes:
Skills to work on:	
Student Name:	Notes:
Skills to work on:	
Student Name:	Notes:
Skills to work on:	
Student Name:	Notes:
Skills to work on:	
Student Name:	Notes:
Skills to work on:	

Lesson Plan

Group:	Date:
Book Title:	**Level:**

Word Work:

Teaching Point/Strategy:	**Vocabulary:**

Before Reading:

During Reading:

After Reading:

Other:

Notes

Student Name:	Notes:
Skills to work on:	
Student Name:	Notes:
Skills to work on:	
Student Name:	Notes:
Skills to work on:	
Student Name:	Notes:
Skills to work on:	
Student Name:	Notes:
Skills to work on:	

Lesson Plan

Group:	Date:

Book Title:	Level:

Word Work:

Teaching Point/Strategy:	Vocabulary:

Before Reading:

During Reading:

After Reading:

Other:

Notes

Student Name:	Notes:
Skills to work on:	
Student Name:	Notes:
Skills to work on:	
Student Name:	Notes:
Skills to work on:	
Student Name:	Notes:
Skills to work on:	
Student Name:	Notes:
Skills to work on:	

Lesson Plan

Group:	Date:
Book Title:	**Level:**

Word Work:

Teaching Point/Strategy:	Vocabulary:

Before Reading:

During Reading:

After Reading:

Other:

Notes

Student Name: Skills to work on:	Notes:
Student Name: Skills to work on:	Notes:
Student Name: Skills to work on:	Notes:
Student Name: Skills to work on:	Notes:
Student Name: Skills to work on:	Notes:

Lesson Plan

Group: Date:

Book Title: Level:

Word Work:

Teaching Point/Strategy: Vocabulary:

Before Reading:

During Reading:

After Reading:

Other:

Notes

Student Name: Skills to work on:	Notes:
Student Name: Skills to work on:	Notes:
Student Name: Skills to work on:	Notes:
Student Name: Skills to work on:	Notes:
Student Name: Skills to work on:	Notes:

Lesson Plan

Group:	Date:

Book Title:	Level:

Word Work:

Teaching Point/Strategy:	Vocabulary:

Before Reading:

During Reading:

After Reading:

Other:

Notes

Student Name: Skills to work on:	Notes:
Student Name: Skills to work on:	Notes:
Student Name: Skills to work on:	Notes:
Student Name: Skills to work on:	Notes:
Student Name: Skills to work on:	Notes:

Lesson Plan

Group: Date:

Book Title: Level:

Word Work:

Teaching Point/Strategy: Vocabulary:

Before Reading:

During Reading:

After Reading:

Other:

Notes

Student Name:	Notes:
Skills to work on:	
Student Name:	Notes:
Skills to work on:	
Student Name:	Notes:
Skills to work on:	
Student Name:	Notes:
Skills to work on:	
Student Name:	Notes:
Skills to work on:	

Lesson Plan

Group:	Date:

Book Title: Level:

Word Work:

Teaching Point/Strategy: Vocabulary:

Before Reading:

During Reading:

After Reading:

Other:

Notes

Student Name: Skills to work on:	Notes:
Student Name: Skills to work on:	Notes:
Student Name: Skills to work on:	Notes:
Student Name: Skills to work on:	Notes:
Student Name: Skills to work on:	Notes:

Lesson Plan

Group:	Date:

Book Title:	Level:

Word Work:

Teaching Point/Strategy:	Vocabulary:

Before Reading:

During Reading:

After Reading:

Other:

Notes

Student Name: Skills to work on:	Notes:
Student Name: Skills to work on:	Notes:
Student Name: Skills to work on:	Notes:
Student Name: Skills to work on:	Notes:
Student Name: Skills to work on:	Notes:

Lesson Plan

Group:	Date:

Book Title: Level:

Word Work:

Teaching Point/Strategy:	Vocabulary:

Before Reading:

During Reading:

After Reading:

Other:

Notes

Student Name: Skills to work on:	Notes:
Student Name: Skills to work on:	Notes:
Student Name: Skills to work on:	Notes:
Student Name: Skills to work on:	Notes:
Student Name: Skills to work on:	Notes:

Lesson Plan

Group: Date:

Book Title: Level:

Word Work:

Teaching Point/Strategy: Vocabulary:

Before Reading:

During Reading:

After Reading:

Other:

Notes

Student Name: Skills to work on:	Notes:
Student Name: Skills to work on:	Notes:
Student Name: Skills to work on:	Notes:
Student Name: Skills to work on:	Notes:
Student Name: Skills to work on:	Notes:

Lesson Plan

Group:	Date:
Book Title:	Level:

Word Work:

Teaching Point/Strategy: **Vocabulary:**

Before Reading:

During Reading:

After Reading:

Other:

Notes

Student Name:	Notes:
Skills to work on:	
Student Name:	Notes:
Skills to work on:	
Student Name:	Notes:
Skills to work on:	
Student Name:	Notes:
Skills to work on:	
Student Name:	Notes:
Skills to work on:	

Lesson Plan

Group:	Date:
Book Title:	**Level:**

Word Work:

Teaching Point/Strategy:	**Vocabulary:**

Before Reading:

During Reading:

After Reading:

Other:

Notes

Student Name:	Notes:
Skills to work on:	
Student Name:	Notes:
Skills to work on:	
Student Name:	Notes:
Skills to work on:	
Student Name:	Notes:
Skills to work on:	
Student Name:	Notes:
Skills to work on:	

Lesson Plan

Group:	Date:
Book Title:	**Level:**

Word Work:

Teaching Point/Strategy:	Vocabulary:

Before Reading:

During Reading:

After Reading:

Other:

Notes

Student Name:	Notes:
Skills to work on:	
Student Name:	Notes:
Skills to work on:	
Student Name:	Notes:
Skills to work on:	
Student Name:	Notes:
Skills to work on:	
Student Name:	Notes:
Skills to work on:	

Lesson Plan

Group:	Date:

Book Title:	Level:

Word Work:

Teaching Point/Strategy:	Vocabulary:

Before Reading:

During Reading:

After Reading:

Other:

Notes

Student Name:	Notes:
Skills to work on:	
Student Name:	Notes:
Skills to work on:	
Student Name:	Notes:
Skills to work on:	
Student Name:	Notes:
Skills to work on:	
Student Name:	Notes:
Skills to work on:	

Lesson Plan

Group:	Date:
Book Title:	Level:

Word Work:

Teaching Point/Strategy:	Vocabulary:

Before Reading:

During Reading:

After Reading:

Other:

Notes

Student Name: Skills to work on:	Notes:
Student Name: Skills to work on:	Notes:
Student Name: Skills to work on:	Notes:
Student Name: Skills to work on:	Notes:
Student Name: Skills to work on:	Notes:

Lesson Plan

Group:	Date:
Book Title:	Level:

Word Work:

Teaching Point/Strategy: | **Vocabulary:**

Before Reading:

During Reading:

After Reading:

Other:

Notes

Student Name:	Notes:
Skills to work on:	
Student Name:	Notes:
Skills to work on:	
Student Name:	Notes:
Skills to work on:	
Student Name:	Notes:
Skills to work on:	
Student Name:	Notes:
Skills to work on:	

Lesson Plan

Group:	Date:

Book Title:	Level:

Word Work:

Teaching Point/Strategy:	Vocabulary:

Before Reading:

During Reading:

After Reading:

Other:

Notes

Student Name: Skills to work on:	Notes:
Student Name: Skills to work on:	Notes:
Student Name: Skills to work on:	Notes:
Student Name: Skills to work on:	Notes:
Student Name: Skills to work on:	Notes:

Lesson Plan

Group:	Date:

Book Title:	Level:

Word Work:

Teaching Point/Strategy:	Vocabulary:

Before Reading:

During Reading:

After Reading:

Other:

Notes

Student Name: Skills to work on:	Notes:
Student Name: Skills to work on:	Notes:
Student Name: Skills to work on:	Notes:
Student Name: Skills to work on:	Notes:
Student Name: Skills to work on:	Notes:

Lesson Plan

Group:	Date:

Book Title:	Level:

Word Work:

Teaching Point/Strategy:	Vocabulary:

Before Reading:

During Reading:

After Reading:

Other:

Notes

Student Name: Skills to work on:	Notes:
Student Name: Skills to work on:	Notes:
Student Name: Skills to work on:	Notes:
Student Name: Skills to work on:	Notes:
Student Name: Skills to work on:	Notes:

Lesson Plan

Group:	Date:
Book Title:	Level:

Word Work:

Teaching Point/Strategy: **Vocabulary:**

Before Reading:

During Reading:

After Reading:

Other:

Notes

Student Name:	Notes:
Skills to work on:	
Student Name:	Notes:
Skills to work on:	
Student Name:	Notes:
Skills to work on:	
Student Name:	Notes:
Skills to work on:	
Student Name:	Notes:
Skills to work on:	

Lesson Plan

Group:	Date:
Book Title:	Level:

Word Work:

Teaching Point/Strategy:	Vocabulary:

Before Reading:

During Reading:

After Reading:

Other:

Notes

Student Name: Skills to work on:	Notes:
Student Name: Skills to work on:	Notes:
Student Name: Skills to work on:	Notes:
Student Name: Skills to work on:	Notes:
Student Name: Skills to work on:	Notes:

Lesson Plan

Group:	Date:
Book Title:	Level:

Word Work:

Teaching Point/Strategy:	Vocabulary:

Before Reading:

During Reading:

After Reading:

Other:

Notes

Student Name:	Notes:
Skills to work on:	
Student Name:	Notes:
Skills to work on:	
Student Name:	Notes:
Skills to work on:	
Student Name:	Notes:
Skills to work on:	
Student Name:	Notes:
Skills to work on:	

Lesson Plan

Group: Date:

Book Title: Level:

Word Work:

Teaching Point/Strategy: Vocabulary:

Before Reading:

During Reading:

After Reading:

Other:

Notes

Student Name:	Notes:
Skills to work on:	
Student Name:	Notes:
Skills to work on:	
Student Name:	Notes:
Skills to work on:	
Student Name:	Notes:
Skills to work on:	
Student Name:	Notes:
Skills to work on:	

Lesson Plan

Group:	Date:
Book Title:	**Level:**

Word Work:

Teaching Point/Strategy:	Vocabulary:

Before Reading:

During Reading:

After Reading:

Other:

Notes

Student Name:	Notes:
Skills to work on:	
Student Name:	Notes:
Skills to work on:	
Student Name:	Notes:
Skills to work on:	
Student Name:	Notes:
Skills to work on:	
Student Name:	Notes:
Skills to work on:	

Lesson Plan

Group:	Date:

Book Title: Level:

Word Work:

Teaching Point/Strategy: **Vocabulary:**

Before Reading:

During Reading:

After Reading:

Other:

Notes

Student Name:	Notes:
Skills to work on:	
Student Name:	Notes:
Skills to work on:	
Student Name:	Notes:
Skills to work on:	
Student Name:	Notes:
Skills to work on:	
Student Name:	Notes:
Skills to work on:	

Lesson Plan

Group:	Date:

Book Title: Level:

Word Work:

Teaching Point/Strategy: **Vocabulary:**

Before Reading:

During Reading:

After Reading:

Other:

Notes

Student Name: Skills to work on:	Notes:
Student Name: Skills to work on:	Notes:
Student Name: Skills to work on:	Notes:
Student Name: Skills to work on:	Notes:
Student Name: Skills to work on:	Notes:

Lesson Plan

Group:	Date:

Book Title:	Level:

Word Work:

Teaching Point/Strategy:	Vocabulary:

Before Reading:

During Reading:

After Reading:

Other:

Notes

Student Name:	Notes:
Skills to work on:	
Student Name:	Notes:
Skills to work on:	
Student Name:	Notes:
Skills to work on:	
Student Name:	Notes:
Skills to work on:	
Student Name:	Notes:
Skills to work on:	

Lesson Plan

Group: Date:

Book Title: Level:

Word Work:

Teaching Point/Strategy: Vocabulary:

Before Reading:

During Reading:

After Reading:

Other:

Notes

Student Name: Skills to work on:	Notes:
Student Name: Skills to work on:	Notes:
Student Name: Skills to work on:	Notes:
Student Name: Skills to work on:	Notes:
Student Name: Skills to work on:	Notes:

Lesson Plan

Group:	Date:

Book Title:	Level:

Word Work:

Teaching Point/Strategy:	Vocabulary:

Before Reading:

During Reading:

After Reading:

Other:

Notes

Student Name:	Notes:
Skills to work on:	
Student Name:	Notes:
Skills to work on:	
Student Name:	Notes:
Skills to work on:	
Student Name:	Notes:
Skills to work on:	
Student Name:	Notes:
Skills to work on:	

Lesson Plan

Group:	Date:
Book Title:	Level:

Word Work:

Teaching Point/Strategy: **Vocabulary:**

Before Reading:

During Reading:

After Reading:

Other:

Notes

Student Name:	Notes:
Skills to work on:	
Student Name:	Notes:
Skills to work on:	
Student Name:	Notes:
Skills to work on:	
Student Name:	Notes:
Skills to work on:	
Student Name:	Notes:
Skills to work on:	

Lesson Plan

Group:	Date:
Book Title:	Level:

Word Work:

Teaching Point/Strategy:	Vocabulary:

Before Reading:

During Reading:

After Reading:

Other:

Notes

Student Name: Skills to work on:	Notes:
Student Name: Skills to work on:	Notes:
Student Name: Skills to work on:	Notes:
Student Name: Skills to work on:	Notes:
Student Name: Skills to work on:	Notes:

Lesson Plan

Group:	Date:

Book Title: Level:

Word Work:

Teaching Point/Strategy:	Vocabulary:

Before Reading:

During Reading:

After Reading:

Other:

Notes

Student Name: Skills to work on:	Notes:
Student Name: Skills to work on:	Notes:
Student Name: Skills to work on:	Notes:
Student Name: Skills to work on:	Notes:
Student Name: Skills to work on:	Notes:

Lesson Plan

Group:	Date:

Book Title: Level:

Word Work:

Teaching Point/Strategy: Vocabulary:

Before Reading:

During Reading:

After Reading:

Other:

Notes

Student Name:	Notes:
Skills to work on:	
Student Name:	**Notes:**
Skills to work on:	
Student Name:	**Notes:**
Skills to work on:	
Student Name:	**Notes:**
Skills to work on:	
Student Name:	**Notes:**
Skills to work on:	

Lesson Plan

Group:	Date:

Book Title:	Level:

Word Work:

Teaching Point/Strategy: **Vocabulary:**

Before Reading:

During Reading:

After Reading:

Other:

Notes

Student Name:	Notes:
Skills to work on:	
Student Name:	Notes:
Skills to work on:	
Student Name:	Notes:
Skills to work on:	
Student Name:	Notes:
Skills to work on:	
Student Name:	Notes:
Skills to work on:	

Lesson Plan

Group:	Date:
Book Title:	**Level:**

Word Work:

Teaching Point/Strategy: | **Vocabulary:**

Before Reading:

During Reading:

After Reading:

Other:

Notes

Student Name: Skills to work on:	Notes:
Student Name: Skills to work on:	Notes:
Student Name: Skills to work on:	Notes:
Student Name: Skills to work on:	Notes:
Student Name: Skills to work on:	Notes:

Lesson Plan

Group:	Date:
Book Title:	Level:

Word Work:

Teaching Point/Strategy:	Vocabulary:

Before Reading:

During Reading:

After Reading:

Other:

Notes

Student Name:	Notes:
Skills to work on:	
Student Name:	Notes:
Skills to work on:	
Student Name:	Notes:
Skills to work on:	
Student Name:	Notes:
Skills to work on:	
Student Name:	Notes:
Skills to work on:	

Lesson Plan

Group:	Date:
Book Title:	Level:

Word Work:

Teaching Point/Strategy:	Vocabulary:

Before Reading:

During Reading:

After Reading:

Other:

Notes

Student Name:	Notes:
Skills to work on:	
Student Name:	Notes:
Skills to work on:	
Student Name:	Notes:
Skills to work on:	
Student Name:	Notes:
Skills to work on:	
Student Name:	Notes:
Skills to work on:	

Lesson Plan

Group:	Date:

Book Title:	Level:

Word Work:

Teaching Point/Strategy:	Vocabulary:

Before Reading:

During Reading:

After Reading:

Other:

Notes

Student Name:	Notes:
Skills to work on:	
Student Name:	Notes:
Skills to work on:	
Student Name:	Notes:
Skills to work on:	
Student Name:	Notes:
Skills to work on:	
Student Name:	Notes:
Skills to work on:	

Lesson Plan

Group:	Date:
Book Title:	Level:

Word Work:

Teaching Point/Strategy:	Vocabulary:

Before Reading:

During Reading:

After Reading:

Other:

Notes

Student Name: Skills to work on:	Notes:
Student Name: Skills to work on:	Notes:
Student Name: Skills to work on:	Notes:
Student Name: Skills to work on:	Notes:
Student Name: Skills to work on:	Notes:

Lesson Plan

Group:	Date:
Book Title:	Level:

Word Work:

Teaching Point/Strategy: Vocabulary:

Before Reading:

During Reading:

After Reading:

Other:

Notes

Student Name:	Notes:
Skills to work on:	
Student Name:	Notes:
Skills to work on:	
Student Name:	Notes:
Skills to work on:	
Student Name:	Notes:
Skills to work on:	
Student Name:	Notes:
Skills to work on:	

Lesson Plan

Group:	Date:

Book Title:	Level:

Word Work:

Teaching Point/Strategy:	Vocabulary:

Before Reading:

During Reading:

After Reading:

Other:

Notes

Student Name: Skills to work on:	Notes:
Student Name: Skills to work on:	Notes:
Student Name: Skills to work on:	Notes:
Student Name: Skills to work on:	Notes:
Student Name: Skills to work on:	Notes:

Lesson Plan

Group: Date:

Book Title: Level:

Word Work:

Teaching Point/Strategy: Vocabulary:

Before Reading:

During Reading:

After Reading:

Other:

Notes

Student Name:	Notes:
Skills to work on:	
Student Name:	Notes:
Skills to work on:	
Student Name:	Notes:
Skills to work on:	
Student Name:	Notes:
Skills to work on:	
Student Name:	Notes:
Skills to work on:	

Made in the USA
Middletown, DE
01 August 2019